AMMA'S LOVE

A POETIC JOURNEY

SATHYARAJ NATARAJAN

Made with ♥ on the Notion Press Platform
www.notionpress.com

This poetry book is dedicated to my mother, who has been my guiding light, my rock, and my inspiration throughout my life. Her love, wisdom, and unwavering support have been the driving force behind my writing, and I am forever grateful for the memories, lessons, and moments that we shared together. This collection of poems is a small tribute to the woman who taught me the true meaning of love, sacrifice, and strength. To my mother, thank you for everything. You will always be in my heart and in my thoughts.

Contents

Contents

Foreword

As I read through the pages of this poetry book, I was struck by the raw emotion and vulnerability that Sathyaraj Natarajan has imbued into each and every verse. Through their powerful and evocative imagery, these poems transport the reader on a journey through the author's deepest thoughts and feelings, delving into the complexities of love, loss, grief, and hope.

It is clear that Sathyaraj has poured their heart and soul into this collection, and the result is a deeply moving and personal exploration of the human experience. Whether it is the tenderness of a mother's love, the pain of losing a loved one, or the hope that comes with the arrival of a new life, each poem is a powerful reflection of the author's unique perspective and voice.

As you read through these pages, I encourage you to take the time to truly absorb the words and let the poems speak to you in your own way. Whether you are experiencing similar emotions or simply looking for a deeper understanding of the human experience, this poetry book is sure to resonate with you on a profound level.

So take a moment to sit back, let go of your distractions, and immerse yourself in this powerful collection of poems. I have no doubt that you will come away from this book feeling deeply moved and inspired.

Preface

As the author of this poetry book, I am honored to present to you a collection of poems that have been deeply personal and meaningful to me. Each poem within these pages is an expression of my emotions, thoughts and memories, depicting the various stages of my life, and the people and experiences that have shaped me.This poetry book is a tribute to my mother, who was a constant source of inspiration and love throughout my life. Her unwavering support, guidance and sacrifice has been the driving force behind the creation of these poems. Each verse is a reflection of the profound impact she has had on me, and the memories that we shared together.Through this poetry book, I have tried to capture the beauty of life, its joys and sorrows,its triumphs and struggles. I hope that these poems will touch your hearts and remind you of the moments that matter most in life.I would like to express my gratitude to all those who have supported me throughout thisjourney, and have helped me bring this poetry book to fruition. I hope you will enjoy reading these poems as much as I have enjoyed writing them.

Acknowledgements

I am deeply grateful to my family, especially my brother Giriraj, his wife Rajasree, my cousin and best friend Rahul, and my editor Anagha K, for their unwavering support and encouragement throughout my journey as a writer. This is my first publication, and I could not have done it without their guidance, motivation and love. Thank you for being my rock and helping me through every situation. My family has always been my support system, and I am so grateful for the love and encouragement they have given me throughout my life. I couldn't have done this without you all. I would also like to thank my editor, Anagha K, for her invaluable insights and guidance. Her expertise and experience helped me to take my writing to the next level, and I am so grateful for her support.Illustration design by Freepik. Finally, I want to express my gratitude to the readers of this poetry book. Your interest and support means the world to me and I hope you enjoy reading these poems as much as I enjoyed writing them.

Prologue

This collection of poetry is a journey through the emotions and experiences that shape our lives. From the joys and triumphs to the sorrows and struggles, these poems explore the human condition in all its complexity. They are a reflection of the author's personal journey, as well as a mirror for the reader's own.

The poems within these pages delve into themes of love, loss, family, and identity, painting a picture of the world and the people within it. They are a reminder that we are all connected, that our struggles and triumphs are universal. They remind us that even in the darkest of times, there is still hope and light to be found.

We invite you to delve into these pages, to explore the words and emotions within, and to find a piece of yourself in these lines. This poetry book is not just the author's story, but also a story of us all.

1. A PRINCE'S WORLD

After coming out of my mother's womb,
I saw the world through her eyes,
Her love and warmth in her smile,
Was my first and greatest prize.
She treated me like a prince,
With care and gentle touch,
Showing me the beauty of the world,
And all that I could be and much
I laughed and played in her arms,
With her love as my guide,
The world was a wonderful place,
In which I could safely reside.
I knew that I was special,
With my mother by my side,
And I knew that I was loved,
With her love as my tide.

2. AMMA'S LOVE

Amma's love was like a river,
Ever-flowing, deep and wide,
It nourished me and kept me safe,
From the moment I was inside.
Amma's arms were my first home,
Where I learned to laugh and play,
She held me tight when I was afraid,
And chased my fears away.
As a child, I was afraid of lightning,
But in Amma's arms, I was safe,
She held me close and whispered softly,
That everything would be okay.
Amma's touch was a balm,
That soothed away my fears,
And I knew that I was loved,
Through the laughter and the tears.
As I grew, I came to see,
That Amma's love was boundless,
It followed me wherever I went,
And gave my life a sense of purpose.

3. AMMA'S HEALING TOUCH

Amma was my doctor,
A healer of the heart,
She nursed me through my childhood,
Whenever I fell apart.
With my health in need of care,
Amma's love was my constant guide,
My protector, my sanctuary.
She held my hand and whispered,
Words of comfort and of hope,
And through her gentle care,
I learned to overcome.
With each new setback and illness,
Amma was always by my side,
Her love and care my medicine,
My strength, my pride.
As I grew older and stronger,
And left Amma's care,
I knew that her love would always be,
A light, a guiding star, always there.

4. A TRIP DOWN MEMORY LANE

Every year we journey,
To the village of my Amma's youth,
Where memories linger,
And stories of her life, unfold
We walk the streets together,
Amma's kin from near and far,
Sharing laughter and joy,
And creating new memories, like a star.
We visit the temple,
And offer our prayers,
Feeling Amma's presence,
In the gentle breeze that airs.
We share a meal together,
And raise a glass to her memory,
A tradition we hold dear,
A family gathering, full of love and cheer.

5. AMMA'S TREATS

When I go shopping with Amma,
We buy groceries and other items,
But my favourite part,
Is when we take the bus together,
And she sits with me, watching over.
Amma always lets me choose,
A treat for myself,
And I always go for the chocolate,
With a smile on my face, feeling
happy and nothing else.
We walk down the aisle,
And Amma holds my hand tight,
Watching over me
, Making sure I'm alright.
I love going shopping with Amma,
It's a special treat,
And I know that no matter what,
Her love will always be sweet.

6. AMMA'S KITCHEN MAGIC

Stepping into Amma's kitchen,
Was like stepping into a dream,
The smells and sounds and colours,
Were always so supreme.
She's always busy with cooking and
And her hands moved with such skill,
Creating dishes that were more than food,
But memories that always will.
Amma loved looking at cooking books,
And trying something new,
All of them were delicious,
And the banana fritters, oh so cool.
Her carrot halwa was my favourite,
A sweet and creamy delight,
But her chapatis and curries too,
Were always a pure delight.
Even now, when I'm grown,
And miles away from home,
I can close my eyes and taste,
Amma's cooking magic all my own.

7. A MOTHER'S TOUCH

Every birthday, Amma would pick me
A dress that fit me just right,
With her gentle touch and keen eye,
She made me feel like a star so bright.
We'd roam the shops and boutiques,
And I'd try on dress after dress,
But none of them felt quite like home,
Until Amma found the one, I must confess.
It was my favourite dress of the year,
Fitting me like a glove,
With Amma's love and care sewn in,
I knew I was truly loved.
Though Amma is no longer here,
Her love lives on through these clothes,
And in these moments, I remember,
Her touch and all she chose.

8. A SAFE HAVEN

Growing up in an orthodox family,
My mother never forced her ways,
Though fights may have occurred,
I remember a peaceful home where
love and understanding reign.
But she knew how to use her words,
To guide and protect me with care,
And I could always tell her anything,
Our friendship was always there.
From love to periods,
No topic was off limits,
And with her by my side,
I never felt any distance.
She was my safe haven,
A constant source of love and support,
And though she's no longer here,
Her guidance and wisdom will
always be a comfort.

9. THE MAGIC OF AMMA

There is a special magic,
That lies within a mother,
The way she handles her children,
Is like no other.
All children are drawn to her,
As if by an unseen force,
They play and laugh with her,
And become one, of course.
Amma's touch, her laughter,
Her gentle words and care,
Create a bond so strong,
That it's impossible to compare.
It's a sight to behold,
The love between a mother and child,
And in those moments,
The magic of Amma, runs wild.

10. THE SOUND OF AMMA'S VOICE

The sound of Amma's voice,
Soft and soothing in my ear,
A lullaby to calm my fears,
And chase away any tear.
I remember as a child,
Snuggled safe and warm in bed,
Amma's voice a constant guide,
As she whispered stories in my head.
And as I grew and faced the world,
Amma's voice was still my guide,
A beacon in the darkest times,
A light to help me find my way inside.
Now, even though she's gone,
Amma's voice still echoes in my heart,
A reminder of her love and care,
That will never, ever depart.

11. A WARRIOR'S STRENGTH

After my father's passing,
My mother faced those moments with grace,
With nothing but her love to guide us,
She took our hands and led the way.
Through tears and struggles,
She bravely carried on,
And slowly but surely,
She rebuilt our broken home.
With her strength and determination,
She brought us back to life,
And we watched in awe,
As she transformed into a warrior,
fighting for her family's rights.
Hat's off to my mother,
For her unwavering love and courage,
And to my brother, who played a crucial role,
In helping us to heal and move forward.

12. A JOURNEY THROUGH GRIEF

We set out on a difficult journey,
To spread my father's ashes in Badrinath.
My mother and I took a train,
While my brother flew in from another station.
Excited for our first AC train ride,
And the sights of North India
we'd never seen before.
But as we arrived in Delhi, the
heat was unbearably hot,
Turns out,the extreme heat had
made her dizzy and she fell,
We were shocked and no one
around even looked back.
We somehow got an auto rickshaw
and went to a hospital,
But in the chaos, my mother's bag,
purse and phone were lost.
But after some rest and treatment,
she was discharged.
At the airport, they refused to
let us board the flight,
My mother was exhausted and my

brother and I argued with them.
But my cousin came to the rescue
and booked another flight,
So, my mother and I flew to Chennai,
my brother to Kochi, what a plight.
It was my first flight, I was scared
and my ears closed,
But the air hostess was kind and my
mother said she had a great time.
Though the journey was cut short,
we still carried my father's memory,
And returned home, with a different
experience and a heavy heart's symphony.

13. MISSING AMMA

After my father's passing,
I left home to continue my studies,
But every night before bed,
I'd close my eyes and miss Amma's
warmth and love.
Her gentle words and her touch,
Were a comfort in the darkest of days,
And though miles separated us,
Her presence always found its way.
I longed for her hugs and her laughter,
And the way she'd tuck me in at night,
But even though I was away,
Amma's love shined ever so bright.

14. MOTHER'S SACRIFICE

For us, Amma suffered through days,
Making sacrifices without a single complain,
Working hard to provide for her children's,
And always putting us before her own gain.
Though her own dreams may
have been put on hold,
She never once let us see her pain,
And through her selflessness and love,
She showed us the true meaning of
strength and sustenance.
We may not have had all the luxuries,
But we always had Amma's love,
And in that love, we found true wealth,
A treasure more precious than any above.
Though she may not be with us now,
Her love and sacrifice will forever remain,
A shining example of a mother's love,
And a guiding light through
life's constant refrain.

15. A SPECIAL CONNECTION

Amma's bond with Girimon,
It Is something truly special to see,
They may not always speak in words,
But their love is plain as can be.
I may feel a twinge of jealousy,
When I see how close they are,
But watching them together,
Fills my heart with shining stars.
Their conversations may be brief,
But the love they share is deep,
And even when my brother's not around,
I know Amma will always keep.
Their bond is unbreakable,
A love that will always last,
And though I may be envious,
It's a love I'll forever cherish and hold fast.

16. REBUILDING TOGETHER

In the wake of my father's passing
My brother and Amma picked up the pieces
, And together we built a new world,
From the ashes of our old to new releases.
With their love and guidance,
We found strength and hope,
And slowly but surely,
We built a life that could cope.
From zero to heaven,
We created a new home,
And in this world,
I've never felt alone.
With my brother and Amma by my side,
I know that anything is possible,
Together we can build a life,
That is truly remarkable.

17. A QUALITY TO ADMIRE

My mother has a way with people,
She quickly becomes close with all,
Her gentle nature and kind heart,
Makes her loved by one and all.
Watching her interact with children,
I am filled with admiration and pride,
For I too wish to possess that quality,
To be gentle and open-minded.
But not everything can be the same,
And that's okay, for my mother's touch,
Is a gift, one that will always be cherished,
In the hearts of those she's loved so much.

18. LESSONS LEARNED

My mother's life lessons have been countless,
Even when I didn't understand at the time,
I often realize their worth later on,
Her wisdom and guidance forever in my mind.
She taught me the value of hard work,
And the importance of kindness and empathy,
Her unwavering love and support,
Shaped me into the person I am today.
Though she's no longer here,
Her teachings live on in my heart,
Guiding me through life's challenges,
And giving me the strength to start.
I am grateful for every lesson,
That my mother has taught me,
And I will always carry them,
As a part of my legacy.

19. RIDING WITH AMMA

Bike rides with my mother,
My best riding partner,
No matter the distance,
She always wants to go further.
From the temples to the relatives' houses,
To friends' homes and beyond,
Amma finds joy in every journey,
And I am so grateful for her bond.
We stop for juice and food,
Trying different places,
Some may say mothers should take it slow,
But not Amma, she's always ready to go,
With her by my side,
The journey is beautiful,
And I'm grateful for every ride,
With my dear mother, Amma.

20. FRIENDSHIP AND SISTERHOOD

When mother and her friends get together,
They laugh and chat for hours on end,
Sharing stories and memories,
Their bond a true and cherished friend.
They swap recipes and give advice,
And offer a listening ear,
Their laughter echoes through the house,
Filling it with love and cheer.
I watch them from a distance,
Feeling grateful for their friendship,
For the way they lift my mother's spirits,
And bring her joy and happiness.
Their bond is one of sisterhood,
A bond that will never break,
And I'm grateful to be a part of it,
Through the laughter and the heartache.

21. BOND OF GENERATIONS

Mother and daughter,
My mother's mother, my grandmother,
Their bond is truly special,
Full of stories and memories.
A mutual love shines through,
No fights or conflicts to be found,
Each visit brings joy and gifts,
A bond so rare and profound.
Not only between them,
But with all of mother's siblings,
Their bond of generations,
Is one that truly glimmers.

22. A NEW BEGINNING

My heart was broken, my mind in despair,
A love lost, a future unclear,
But in the darkness, my mother was there,
With open arms and a listening ear.
She understood my pain and my fears,
And held me tight through all my cries,
With her gentle words and her loving care,
She helped me see the light in my eyes.
I struggled to pick up the pieces,
To find my way out of the dark,
But with my mother by my side,
I knew I would make a fresh start.
She gave me the strength to move on,
To leave the past behind,
And with her love and her guidance,
I found a new beginning to find.
I may not have the words to express,
The depth of gratitude I hold,
But I know that I wouldn't be here,
If it weren't for my mother's love to behold

23. RISING FROM THE FLOOD

The flood came sudden, like a thief in the night
Our home submerged, an unimaginable sight
But Amma stood strong, a rock through it all
Calm and collected, she didn't let us fall
Though everything we knew was swept away,
She showed us how to start anew each day.
With calm and grace, she cleared the debris,
And slowly, hope returned to
our hearts, you'll see.
Amma taught us that in life, we must roll,
With the punches, and never lose control.
For just like the flood, that came and went,
We too, can rise and make a brand-new start.
And though our home may be different now,
The love and warmth of family
will always be around.
Thanks to Amma's strength, we're standing tall,
And ready to face whatever comes, one and all.

24. QUARANTINE COOKING WITH AMMA

Trapped inside our home,
the world in chaos and fear,
But Amma's love was a constant,
always near.
She cooked up a storm, experimenting with
flair, and shared her creations,
with love and care.
From porotta to biriyani, her skills on
full display, Each dish a reflection,
of her heart's true way. She brought us comfort,
in a time of uncertainty, Her cooking,
a reminder, of her boundless generosity.
We spent our days, chatting and laughing,
With Amma by our side,
we knew we'd be alright.
We ate well and had plenty to share,
and spent time with my grandma next
door Amma would go and visit her
They'd talk and walk, the bond so pure
Though the quarantine may be over,
Amma's love and cooking will forever linger.
A reminder of the bond we share,

And the warmth of home,
that will always be there.

25. THE WEDDING BLISS

Brother's wedding came like a surprise, In the
midst of a pandemic that brought no ties.
But love knows no bounds, and so it was set,
A date chosen, preparations made,
we couldn't fret. Mother beamed
with joy, as she helped with
the plans, from dresses to decor,
she lent her helping hands.
Excitement filled the air, as the day
drew near, my mother's happiness,
I held dear. The day finally arrived,
and we all dressed in our best, the love
between my brother and his bride,
truly blessed. My mother watched
on, with a heart full of
pride, for her son's happiness, she had
always strived. The wedding was beautiful,
and the memories will last, my mother's
joy, forever etched in the past. As we came
back home, I saw her smile with
satisfaction, for in giving her son's
happiness, she found her own elation.

26. THE DARK DAY

A dark day it was,
when our lives changed in a flash,
my sister went away to UK, and my brother too,
with a dash.
But little did we know, that fate had more in
store, for my mother fell ill,
and our hearts were
sore. With a fried stomach,
breathing difficulties
and gas, We went for a check-up,
and the news was crass. The doctor
took me aside, and said the words so clear,
"Your mother has cancer, "
and my heart filled with fear.
We spent a week in the hospital, undergoing
tests, Confirming the diagnosis,
and our hearts filled with unrest.
I had to tell my mother,
and find the strength to say,
"We'll fight this together, in every single way.
" She was not afraid of the cancer,
but of the stage and state,
she was going through it all,
and it was not fate. But we stood strong together,

and fought with all our might,
and though the journey was hard,
we saw the light. Through the dark day,
we held on tight, with love and courage,
we saw the light. And though we may stumble,
we'll rise again, For my mother,
my hero, my closest friend.

27. SURVIVING THE STORM

The dark days came, like a storm,
mother fell ill, her health torn.
Cancer was the diagnosis, and treatment
was the only option for us.
Chemotherapy brought pain
and swelling, but my mother's
strength was never diminishing.
Through the hair loss and abdominal pain,
she held on, never once complaining.
Surgery was next, a daunting task,
but my mother faced it with courage and class.
In the waiting room,
I prayed and hoped, for my mother's health
to be restored and cope.
After the surgery, my mother was weak,
but her love and care still shone so unique.
"Did you eat?"
she asked with concern,
even in her state,
her love for me still burned.
The days in the hospital were long,
but my mother's strength and

will to survive was strong.
She recovered and came back home,
and with each day, her health did roam.
We went for walks, and shared stories,
and in those moments,
our bond was a glory.
My mother's fight and survival,
Was a reminder of a love that's unrivalled.

28. THE ARRIVAL OF A NEW GENERATION

And as the days went by, the news came.
A bundle of joy, a new life to claim.
Mother's heart filled with happiness
and pride, as her child becomes a parent,
her joy multiplied.
The treatment may be tough,
but hope is insight,
as a new generation takes flight.
Brother and sister, excited for the arrival,
A new chapter in life, a new survival.
Mother's love knows no bounds,
as her family expands and surrounds.
With love and joy in every step,
together they face the future,
with no regrets.
A new beginning, a new hope,
As they welcome the child and cope.
Mother's love shines bright,
Guiding them through the darkest night.

29. NORMAL DAYS

So those days went on and on,
Mother and I, hand in hand,
walking in the evening's light,
Sharing stories, deep and grand.
In the evenings, I would cook,
Mother would guide me through,
Sister on video call at night,
we'd talk and laugh, it was true.
After taking medicine with care,
Mother would sleep sound and deep,
Days passed by, with their fair share,
of joy and sorrows to keep.
But through it all, one thing stayed true,
The love of a mother,
pure and true.
A guiding light, in every step,
Memories of a mother's love, to last.

30. THE RETURN OF THE STORM

The storm had come back once again,
bringing with it pain and fear.
Mother received the news with a heavy heart,
As the cancer had reappeared.
We walked in silence, on the path we knew,
As the weight of the news sunk in.
Mother's strength and courage,
reminded me to stay strong within.
We discussed the plans with brother,
And the doctor's date was set.
We prepared for battle, once more,
With a heavy heart and aching head.
But through it all, mother's love,
Shone like a beacon in the dark.
Guiding us through the storm,
once more, with a strength that left a mark
Though the road ahead was uncertain,
we knew we had to fight.
With mother by our side,
everything would be alright.

31. FAREWELL, DEAR AMMA

The balance starts to sway,
Vomiting, unable to eat,
Blood pressure on the rise,
Admitted in emergency.
Tests and checks once more,
now in the brain, the cancer roars.
Tired and worn, my mother and I,
No solution, no reason why.
Radiotherapy starts anew,
But the cancer spreads, it's true.
Sight and hearing start to fade,
Seizures, closer to the final grade.
In the ICU, we wait and pray,
but exhaustion takes its toll each day.
The doctor's words, a heavy weight,
"Prepare, she won't last much more, fate."
Silent in the evening's light,
Oxygen and pressure, out of sight.
All I could do was watch and grieve,
as my dear mother, I had to leave.
Eyes filled with tears, heart heavy and sore,
I bid farewell to my dear mother once

more. Ambulance ride home,
a blur and a dream,
Losing my mother,
a pain supreme.

32. ECHOES OF LOSS

In silence, I roam this empty house,
Memories of you, my dear Amma,
douse My mind in echoes of what once was,
The pain of your loss, a constant buzz.
I am tired, my heart heavy with grief,
As I struggle to find relief,
From the darkness that now surrounds,
And the emptiness that I've found.
Your absence is felt in every room,
And the memories of you,
a constant gloom.
I am lost without you, my guiding light,
in this darkness, I cannot find my sight.
But I will hold on to the love we shared,
And the memories that will always be there,
for in my heart, you will always stay,
Until we meet again, on a brighter day.

33. LOST WITHOUT YOU

Without you, Amma,
I am lost In a world that's spinning fast
Without your guiding hand I am adrift,
forever cast Memories of you linger
on In every corner of my home
But the silence is deafening ,
As I'm left here all alone
I can't bear this pain inside Of losing you,
my rock, my guide I don't know what to do
next Without you by my side You lived for me,
and I for you But now that you're gone,
what can I do?
My heart is broken,
my soul is torn I am lost without
you the darkness fills me,
and I am tired but your love will always be
my guiding fire Though you're gone,
you will live on in every beat of my heart's desire.

34. UNFULFILLED DREAMS

A mother's love, a guiding light ,
Always there to make things right
But now she's gone, and we're left to cope
With dreams unfulfilled and an endless hope
The laughter of her grandchild's cries
The family gatherings, the loving ties
All the things she'll never see
Leaves our hearts with a painful plea
The house she longed to call her own
The joys of our lives, now unknown
A job well done, a life fulfilled
But mother's gone, and our hearts are stilled
The temples she dreamed of visiting
The places she longed to see
But now she's gone, and all that's left
Is the memory of what could have been
Though mother's gone,
her love remains
In the memories and pain
We'll keep her dreams alive
As we go on with our lives.

35. GOGO WILL MISS GRANDMA

Our child, my Gogo,
my brother's baby Kunjigirimon,
my sister's Achu,
Will miss a good friend,
a playful ally A grandmother
who showered love like an ocean
blue Mother's absence,
a gaping hole Filled with memories,
love, and sorrow Gogo's laughter,
now a distant echo A future without her,
we'll have to borrow Perhaps the one who
will miss her the most Is the little one,
who knew her love and grace But now,
she's gone, Leaving us with a longing
embrace The child will grow,
but the memories will stay Of a mother
who loved and left too soon In our hearts,
she'll forever stay As we sing her
praises, under the moon.

36. A Letter To My Dear Amma

My dearest Ammikutty,
I am writing this letter to you with a heavy heart, as I still cannot believe that you are no longer with us. Your absence has left a gaping hole in our lives and we all miss youdearly.I remember the days when you were by my side, always there to guide me and support me. through all of life's challenges. You taught me the true meaning of love and sacrifice,and I will forever be grateful for all that you have done for me. I am so sorry that you had to suffer through the pain of your illness. But I know that youwere strong, and fought until the very end. I am proud of you, and I know that you are now at peace. I want you to know that I will always cherish the memories we shared together. The times we laughed, the times we cried, the times we hugged and the times we kissed. You will always hold a special place in my heart, and I will continue to love and miss you until the end of my days. I know that you are now watching over us, and I take comfort in knowing that you are nolonger in pain. I will always remember the lessons you taught me, and I promise to make you proud.
Rest in peace, my dear mother. I love you.
Your loving child,
Amabadi .. Sathyaraj

About The Author

Sathyaraj Natarajan

Sathyaraj Natarajan, a VFX artist with a creative vision and a passion for all thingsrelated to cinema,technology,and science. As a resident of the small town of Piravom in Ernakulam, Kerala, India, Sathyaraj brings a unique perspective to his craft.Sathyaraj's love for visual effects began at a young age and has only grown strongerover time. He is constantly seeking new ways to push the boundaries of what ispossible in the world of VFX and is always on the lookout for exciting projects to work on.In addition to his work in the film industry, Sathyaraj is also an avid reader and has developed a passion for writing. He plans to explore this passion further in the future, by writing various types of books.When Sathyaraj is not working, he can be found exploring the mysteries of the universe through astronomy, or with his nose buried in a good book. He is always eager to connect and collaborate with other professionals in the industry.

Instagram&Twitter : thisissamayah

Email: thisissamayah@gmail.com

9 798889 517276